MERRY CHRISTMAS

A Victorian Verse

illustrated by Mary Teichman

HarperCollins*Publishers*

Merry Christmas
A Victorian Verse
Illustrations copyright © 1993 by Mary Teichman
Printed in the U.S.A. All rights reserved.

Library of Congress Cataloging-in-Publication Data
    Merry Christmas : a Victorian verse / illustrated by Mary Teichman.
        p.   cm.
    Summary: Describes what each letter in the phrase "Merry Christmas"
stands for, from "M for the Music, merry and clear" to "S for St. Nicholas—
joy of the year!"
    ISBN 0-06-022889-X. — ISBN 0-06-022892-X (lib. bdg.)
    1. Christmas—Juvenile poetry.   2. Children's poetry, American.
[1. Christmas—Poetry.   2. American Poetry.]   I. Teichman, Mary, ill.
PS991.A1M47   1993   92-29870
811'.4—dc20   CIP
                                                          AC

Typography by Christine Hoffman
1   2   3   4   5   6   7   8   9   10
❖
First Edition

For my mother, with love
—M.T.

M for the Music,
merry and clear;

E for the Eve,
the crown of the year;

R for the Romping
of bright girls and boys;

R for the Reindeer
that bring them the toys;

Y for the Yule log
softly aglow.

C for the Cold
of the sky and the snow;

H for the Hearth
where they hang up the hose;

R for the Reel
which the old folks propose;

I for the Icicles
seen through the pane;

S for the Sleigh bells,
with tinkling refrain;

T for the Tree
with gifts all abloom;

M for the Mistletoe
hung in the room;

A for the Anthems
we all love to hear;

S for St. Nicholas—
joy of the year!

MERRY

CHRISTMAS